D1457901

Written by
Kathleen Hex

Editors: Regina Hurh Kim/Gillian Snoddy
Cover Illustrator: Rick Grayson
Cover Designer: Rebekah O. Lewis
Production: Karen Nguyen
Art Director: Moonhee Pak
Project Director: Stacey Faulkner

Table of Contents

Introduction

The main objective of *Grammar Minutes Grade 5* is grammar proficiency, attained by teaching students to apply grammar skills to answer questions effortlessly and rapidly. The questions in this book provide students with practice in the following key areas of fifth-grade grammar instruction:

- nouns
- verbs
- pronouns
- adjectives
- adverbs
- prepositional phrases
- types of sentences

- sentence structure
- appositives and clauses
- noun and pronoun agreement
- subject and verb agreement
- negatives
- prefixes and suffixes
- Greek and Latin roots

Use this comprehensive resource to improve your students' overall grammar proficiency, which will promote greater self-confidence in their grammar skills as well as provide the everyday practice necessary to succeed in testing situations.

Grammar Minutes Grade 5 features 100 "Minutes." Each Minute consists of 10 questions for students to complete within a short time period. As students are becoming familiar with the format of the Minutes, they may need more time to complete each one. Once they are comfortable and familiar with the format, give students a one- to two-minute period to complete each Minute. The quick, timed format, combined with instant feedback, makes this a challenging and motivational assignment that offers students an ongoing opportunity to improve their own proficiency in a manageable, nonthreatening way.

How to Use This Book

Grammar Minutes Grade 5 is designed to generally progress through the skills as they are introduced in the classroom in fifth grade. The Minutes can be implemented in either numerical order, starting with Minute 1, or in any order based on your students' specific needs during the school year. The complexity of the sentences and the tasks within each skill being covered gradually increase so that the first Minute of a skill is generally easier than the second Minute on the same skill. Review lessons are included throughout the book, as well as in an application section at the end of the book.

Grammar Minutes Grade 5 can be used in a variety of ways. Use one Minute a day as a warm-up activity, skill review, assessment, test prep, extra credit assignment, or homework assignment. Keep in mind that students will get the most benefit from each Minute if they receive immediate feedback.

If you use the Minute as a timed activity, begin by placing the paper facedown on the students' desks or displaying it as a transparency. Use a clock or kitchen timer to measure one minute—or more if needed. As the Minutes become more advanced, use your discretion on extending the time frame to several minutes if needed. Encourage students to concentrate on completing each question successfully and not to dwell on questions they cannot complete. At the end of the allotted time, have the students stop working. Read the answers from the answer key (pages 108–112) or display them on a transparency. Have students correct their own work and record their scores on the Minute Journal reproducible (page 6). Then have the class go over each question together to discuss the answers. Spend more time on questions that were clearly challenging for most of the class. Tell students that some skills that seemed difficult for them will appear again on future Minutes and that they will have another opportunity for success.

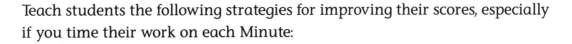

Teach students the following strategies for improving their scores, especially if you time their work on each Minute:

- leave more challenging items for last
- come back to items they are unsure of after they have completed all other items
- make educated guesses when they encounter items with which they are unfamiliar
- ask questions if they are still unsure about anything

Students will ultimately learn to apply these strategies to other assignments and testing situations.

The Minutes are designed to assess and improve grammar proficiency and should not be included as part of a student's overall language arts grade. However, the Minutes provide an excellent opportunity to identify which skills the class as a whole needs to practice or review. Use this information to plan the content of future grammar lessons. For example, if many students in the class have difficulty with a Minute on commas, additional lessons in that area will be useful and valuable for the students' future success.

While Minute scores should not be included in students' formal grades, it is important to recognize student improvements by offering individual or class rewards and incentives for scores above a certain level on a daily and/ or weekly basis. Showing students recognition for their efforts provides additional motivation to succeed.

Minute Journal

Name _____

Minute	Date	Score	Minute	Date	Score	Minute	Date	Score	Minute	Date	Score
1			26			51			76		
2			27			52			77		
3			28			53			78		
4			29			54			79		
5			30			55			80		
6			31			56			81		
7			32			57			82		
8			33			58			83		
9			34			59			84		
10			35			60			85		
11			36			61			86		
12			37			62			87		
13			38			63			88		
14			39			64			89		
15			40			65			90		
16			41			66			91		
17			42			67			92		
18			43			68			93		
19			44			69			94		
20			45			70			95		
21			46			71			96		
22			47			72			97		
23			48			73			98		
24			49			74			99		
25			50			75			100		

6

Grammar Minutes · Grade 5 © 2009 Creative Teaching Press

Scope and Sequence

Minute 1

Name _____

Write *C* if the sentence is complete or *I* if it is incomplete.

1. Mom and Dad froze when they saw the mess in the garage. _____

2. Wonder why Jonas pulled the pickles from the shelf? _____

3. The first thing to do. _____

4. The oven was not hot enough to cook the casserole. _____

5. In all of the nicely decorated rooms. _____

6. At the end of the show, everyone cheered for Darla. _____

7. Imaginary lines that run east and west. _____

8. The dress rehearsal for the concert is Thursday night. _____

9. The rooster pecked furiously at the seeds. _____

10. A light in the lonely attic. _____

Minute 2

Name _____

For Numbers 1–5, underline the simple subject of each sentence.
(**Hint**: The *simple subject* is the someone or something the sentence is about. Example: The neighborhood <u>dogs</u> barked loudly.)

1. Ella walked to the store.

2. Giant squid grow 20 to 60 feet in length.

3. The night stars shine brightly.

4. The Petronas Towers in Kuala Lumpur rise over 1,400 feet.

5. In the office, the phones rang loudly.

For Numbers 6–10, circle the simple predicate of each sentence.
(**Hint**: The *simple predicate* is the action or <u>linking verb</u> without any other words that modify it or describe the subject. Example: The view (overlooked) the ocean.)

6. The famous artist Vincent Van Gogh painted *Sunflowers* in 1888.

7. *Shrek* is Hannah's favorite movie.

8. Trees sway gently in the breeze.

9. The Caldecott Medal is awarded each year to the best picture book.

10. A very sleepy Tyler came down the stairs to eat breakfast.

Grammar Minutes · Grade 5 © 2009 Creative Teaching Press

Simple Subjects and Predicates

Minute 3

Name _____

For Numbers 1–5, underline the complete subject of each sentence.
(**Hint**: The *complete subject* includes all words related to whom or what the sentence is about. Example: <u>A crowded group of people</u> stood in line for the bus.)

1. My sister Lindsey opened her umbrella.

2. The brand-new building was painted bright blue.

3. Alex's sister sliced the bread.

4. The elementary school students guessed how many buttons were in the jar.

5. The eager group of tourists watched the wild animals roam around the African savannah.

For Numbers 6–10, circle the complete predicate for each sentence below.
(**Hint**: The *complete predicate* includes all words that show what the complete subject is or does. Example: A crowded group of people (stood in line for the bus.))

6. Kevin put his books in my backpack.

7. Downhill snow skiing is a fun winter sport.

8. The spring rains helped the flowers bloom.

9. After ringing up my purchase, the cashier politely handed me my receipt.

10. If the conductor is sick, Kate will take her place.

Grammar Minutes • Grade 5 © 2009 Creative Teaching Press

Minute 4

Name _____

For Numbers 1–5, underline the compound subject in each sentence.
(**Hint**: A *compound subject* has two or more simple subjects with the same predicate.
Example: A <u>man</u> and a <u>child</u> walked down the street.)

1. Gretchen and Thelma wandered through the park.

2. In the garden, roses and daisies were blooming all around us.

3. Sweaters, coats, and rugs are often made with wool.

4. The guard and the center worked together to keep the ball away from the opponents.

5. The United States, Canada, and Mexico are in North America.

For Numbers 6–10, write another verb to create a compound predicate for each sentence.
(**Hint**: A *compound predicate* has two or more predicates. Example: A man <u>ate</u> his sandwich and <u>threw</u> the wrapper away.)

6. Marianna washed the dishes and _____ the countertops.

7. The happy babies _____ and played in the bath.

8. Victor _____ music and played video games on his computer.

9. Owen feeds the horses, chickens, and pigs and _____ out the stables.

10. Every morning I eat breakfast, make my lunch, and _____ my school bag.

Compound Subjects and Predicates

Minute 5

Name _____

For Numbers 1–4, circle the exclamatory sentence and underline the interrogative sentence.
(**Hint**: An *exclamatory* sentence shows strong feeling. An *interrogative* sentence asks a question.)

1. Look at that! Isn't that a gorgeous sunset?

2. I can't believe I missed the bus! What will I do now?

3. Was that your fastest swim record? It's unbelievable!

4. I can't believe it's broken! How long will it be before we can get it repaired?

For Numbers 5–7, insert correct end punctuation for each group of sentences.

5. Oh no ___ Sandra hurt her foot ___ Should she go to the doctor ___

6. Wow, look at the size of the trout ___ Is that the biggest fish you've ever caught ___

7. Are you ready ___ Hurry up or we'll be late ___ I think that's the bus ___

For Numbers 8–10, write an exclamatory sentence to fit with each sentence below.

8. _____ What happened to all the peanut butter?

9. _____ I can't concentrate.

10. _____ It is the best cupcake I've ever had!

Minute 6

Name _____

Write *D* if the sentence is declarative. Write *I* if the sentence is imperative.
(**Hint**: A *declarative* sentence is a statement. An *imperative* sentence makes a request or a command. The "you" does not appear in the sentence but it is understood.)

1. Use the old stick to stir the paint. _____

2. We are learning the names of state capitals in school. _____

3. Draw a straight line from A to B. _____

4. Wear a sweater. _____

5. You are really friendly. _____

6. Lower the volume, please. _____

7. The dangerous substances were locked in Mrs. Tipper's science cupboard. _____

8. Use a pointer to indicate the correct coordinates on the map. _____

9. Board the bus before it leaves. _____

10. It is important that the doctor confirms the diagnosis. _____

Grammar Minutes · Grade 5 © 2009 Creative Teaching Press

Minute 7

Name _____

Write the correct end punctuation (period, question mark, or exclamation point) for each sentence.

1. Satellites orbit around a planet ___

2. What's in the box ___

3. I enjoy the smell of ripening peaches ___

4. That is an amazing magic trick ___

5. Who is the boy wearing the purple shoes ___

6. Penguins cannot fly ___

7. You did a great job ___

8. Go get your jacket ___

9. Shannon will be the class president ___

10. What are you having for lunch ___

Grammar Minutes · Grade 5 © 2009 Creative Teaching Press

Minute 8

Name _____

Read each sentence. If it is a complete sentence, add the correct end punctuation mark. If it is an incomplete sentence, write *I* on the line.

1. Always wear a helmet when riding your bike or skateboard _____

2. Our teacher realized we were all beginning violin students _____

3. The meteorologist predicts the weather with great accuracy _____

4. The movie theater on N. Harbor Blvd _____

5. In the past, plantations grew cotton and tobacco _____

6. The money in my savings account for a new bicycle _____

7. Mr. Leonard Wallace Jr., the nicest neighbor on our street _____

8. When people enter the U.S., they are required to present a passport _____

9. All the time _____

10. In a seat aboard a private jet _____

Complete Sentences Review

Grammar Minutes · Grade 5 © 2009 Creative Teaching Press

Minute 9

Name _____

Write *S* if the phrase is a subject or *P* if the phrase is a predicate.

1. many people   _____

2. build their nests on the ground near a body of water   _____

3. is the study of outer space   _____

4. painted the ceiling of the Sistine Chapel in Rome   _____

5. would be a great adventure   _____

6. all of the renewable resources   _____

7. as she walked home from school, Taylor   _____

8. met at the park to practice for Saturday's game   _____

9. Hillary and her family   _____

10. escaped from chains and straightjackets as part of his act   _____

Grammar Minutes • Grade 5 © 2009 Creative Teaching Press

Minute 10

Name _____

For Numbers 1–5, circle the simple subject and underline the complete subject of each sentence.

1. A virus is a microscopic organism.

2. The Great Egyptian Pyramids were built as tombs.

3. My good friends Heather and Tony were the stars of the show.

4. The bright red robin sat on the branch of the tree.

5. The steaming hot chocolate warmed our chilly bones.

For Numbers 6–10, rewrite the sentence to include a compound predicate.

6. Martin walked to school.

    _____

7. All plants use oxygen and water.

    _____

8. My mother curled her hair.

    _____

9. Many Brazilians love to play soccer.

    _____

10. Rachel strolled along the boardwalk.

    _____

Grammar Minutes · Grade 5 © 2009 Creative Teaching Press

Minute 11

Name _____

Insert the correct punctuation at the end of each sentence. Then write the type of sentence it is on the line. Write *D* for declarative, *I* for interrogative, *IMP* for imperative, or *E* for exclamatory.

1. Matter is anything that takes up space ___ _____

2. Dad, can you help me build a birdhouse ___ _____

3. I won one million dollars ___ _____

4. Think about it carefully ___ _____

5. Did someone lose a jacket ___ _____

6. Straighten your tie ___ _____

7. Water boils at 212° Fahrenheit ___ _____

8. How much money do we need ___ _____

9. For the last time, Robert, clean up the mess ___ _____

10. The green notebook is my math notebook ___ _____

Grammar Minutes • Grade 5 © 2009 Creative Teaching Press

Minute 12

Name _____

Write each noun in the box under its correct category.

explorer	city	bucket	friendship
frequently	liberty	park	post office
galloped	shouted	biggest	woman
bread	veterinarian	purple	made

Person	Place	Thing or Idea
1. _____	4. _____	7. _____
2. _____	5. _____	8. _____
3. _____	6. _____	9. _____
		10. _____

Common Nouns

Minute 13

Name _____

Underline the common noun(s) and circle the proper noun(s) in each sentence.
(**Hint:** A *proper noun* names a specific person, place, thing, or idea.)

1. Jeff made a lot of friends at Onondaga Camp.

2. The glove felt just right to Javier.

3. The game took place in Central Park.

4. The students learned about the causes of the Revolutionary War.

5. Steven mixed all the ingredients together.

6. We met at Nick's house before going out to eat.

7. Our science teacher brought us to Hyde's Planetarium.

8. Byron Elementary School has a day off tomorrow.

9. The president of the United States lives in the White House.

10. They studied the pictures of Venus.

Grammar Minutes · Grade 5 © 2009 Creative Teaching Press

Minute 14

Name _____

Circle the proper noun that should be capitalized in each sentence.

1. The official languages in brazil are Portuguese, Spanish, English, and French.

2. Did you know that budapest is the capital of Hungary?

3. Millions of chinese people make a living by farming.

4. The Hindu Festival of Lights is called diwali.

5. The eiffel tower is located in Paris, France.

6. The most important book in Judaism is the torah.

7. There are more than 1 billion muslims in the world.

8. The smallest country in the world is vatican city.

9. My friend juanita, who is from Ecuador, is bilingual.

10. The walt disney concert hall in Los Angeles was opened in October 2003.

Grammar Minutes · Grade 5 © 2009 Creative Teaching Press

Capitalization: Proper Nouns

Minute 15

Name _____

Write the plural form for each noun.
(**Hint:** These plural nouns end in −*s*, −*es,* or -*ies*.)

1. shoe   _____

2. hero   _____

3. box   _____

4. skate   _____

5. monkey   _____

6. company   _____

7. princess   _____

8. cherry   _____

9. witch   _____

10. chimney   _____

Grammar Minutes · Grade 5 © 2009 Creative Teaching Press

Minute 16

Name _____

Circle the two plural nouns in each sentence.
(**Hint:** There are some irregular plurals in these sentences that do not end in –*s,* –*es,* or –*ies*.)

1. The children visited many places on their field trip.

2. They took photos of two deer sipping water from the pond.

3. My grandmother's favorite dishes to make are scalloped potatoes and lemon cream pie.

4. On Thanksgiving Day, our family gets together with other families around our neighborhood to share our blessings and eat dinner.

5. The sheep grazed on the hills, undisturbed by the noise.

6. The paper and pens are on the top two shelves of the supply closet.

7. We raked the leaves into big piles.

8. My friends and I get together at the library to study for our weekly spelling and grammar quizzes.

9. Last December, when my mother and I opened the mall doors, we were greeted by elves.

10. Kevin likes horror movies, but I like biographies.

Minute 17

Name _____

Rewrite each phrase in possessive form.
(**Hint:** Adding 's to a singular noun makes it *possessive*. Example: The pencil belonging to Greg = Greg's pencil.)

1. The web of the spider _____

2. The cookie belonging to Teresa _____

3. The flute belonging to Kenneth _____

4. The lunch belonging to the student _____

5. The stethoscope belonging to the doctor _____

6. The father of the child _____

7. The shoes belonging to Ann _____

8. The legend of the map _____

9. The mascot of the team _____

10. The biography of the writer _____

Grammar Minutes • Grade 5 © 2009 Creative Teaching Press

Minute 18

Name _____

Rewrite each phrase in possessive form.
(**Hint**: A *plural possessive noun* shows ownership by more than one person or thing.
When a plural noun ends in-*s*, adding an apostrophe ['] to the end makes it possessive.
Example: The room belonging to the sisters = sisters' room.)

1. The team of the boys _____

2. The lounge belonging to the teachers _____

3. The captains of the ships _____

4. The computers of the stores _____

5. The classroom of the children _____

6. The dresses belonging to the women _____

7. The projects of the partners _____

8. The colors of the leaves _____

9. The harnesses of the oxen _____

10. The hooves of the deer _____

Plural Possessive Nouns

Minute 19

Name _____

For Numbers 1–5, write a subject pronoun to replace the underlined word or words in each sentence.
(**Hint**: A *subject pronoun* takes the place of one or more nouns in the subject of a sentence. Example: Tae ate hungrily = *He* ate hungrily.)

1. <u>Bill</u> called Conner to ask about the homework assignment. _____

2. <u>The girls</u> changed quickly and went swimming. _____

3. <u>Stella</u> enjoys listening to music on her MP3 player. _____

4. <u>The driver</u> raced around the track at more than 200 miles per hour in his car. _____

5. <u>Our guests</u> stayed for two weeks. _____

For Numbers 6–10, circle the correct object pronoun(s) to complete each sentence.

6. Our principal challenged (we/us) to read 5,000 books this year.

7. Will Cathy go with (she/her) and (me/I) to the skate park?

8. The audience clapped loudly for (us/we).

9. The captains selected (she/her) and (me/I).

10. Mark wanted to buy baseball cards from (him/he) and (me/I).

Grammar Minutes · Grade 5 © 2009 Creative Teaching Press

Minute 20

Name _____

For Numbers 1–5, write the correct reflexive pronoun to complete each sentence.
(**Hint**: A *reflexive* pronoun refers to the subject of the sentence. Use the words ending in *-self* if there is a single subject. Use the words ending in *-selves* for two or more subjects.)

1. I will help _____ to more cake.
   myself   yourselves

2. Each boy should mark _____ present on the attendance list.
   themselves   himself

3. "Lauren and David, make sure to pack some rain gear
   for _____."
   yourself   yourselves

4. The car sat by _____ in the parking lot.
   itself   themselves

5. The teacher said we can talk amongst _____.
   ourselves   ourself

For Numbers 6–10, underline the possessive pronoun(s) in each sentence.
(**Hint**: *Possessive* pronouns show ownership. Example: *Our* house is green.)

6. Devon asked Alice if he could borrow her pencil.

7. Ryan drove to my house quickly and parked his car.

8. Whose papers are on this table?

9. Lasagna is a favorite dish of mine.

10. Your birthday is two days before Lisa's birthday.

Grammar Minutes • Grade 5 © 2009 Creative Teaching Press

Minute 21

Name _____

For Numbers 1–5, use either of the relative pronouns *who* or *that* to correctly complete each sentence.
(**Hint:** Use *who* when referring to a person or *that* if referring to an object or animal.)

1. The customers _____ want a bargain will shop at Pick-n-Pay.

2. The lamp _____ my brother made is purple and yellow.

3. The student _____ has a hearing impairment won an award for bravery.

4. The monkey _____ ate his hat went to the veterinarian.

5. The person _____ is hungriest should eat first.

For Numbers 6–10, circle the indefinite pronoun in each sentence.
(**Hint:** An *indefinite* pronoun does not refer to a specific person, place, or thing.)

6. Anyone can go to the performance on Saturday.

7. There wasn't anything Jackson could have done to prevent the collision.

8. Antonio wants somebody to play tennis with on Thursday.

9. Can everyone see the board?

10. Each of the girls sent a birthday card to Jessica.

Grammar Minutes · Grade 5 © 2009 Creative Teaching Press

Minute 22

Name _____

Write the correct pronoun to complete each sentence.

1. Hybrid cars save gasoline, but _____ more expensive to buy.
                                                  it is   they are

2. Lewis and Clark explored America with _____ corps of volunteers.
                                                his   their

3. Catherine the Great, empress of Russia, expanded _____ empire during her reign.
                  her   their

4. Anybody who loses _____ ticket will not be admitted to the show.
                  their   his

5. Both boys practiced _____ jump shot each night.
                  their   his

6. Something under the bed moved _____ fluffy tail.
                  its   their

7. People should brush _____ teeth twice a day.
                  their   her

8. An electrician must complete extensive training before doing a job on _____ own.
      their   her

9. Campers should be especially careful when _____ near poison oak.
                  they are   she is

10. The first time Wes and Tyson went bowling, _____ each scored over one hundred points.
                  they   he

Noun and Pronoun Agreement

Minute 23

Name _____

Underline the common noun(s) and circle the proper noun(s) in each sentence.

1. When Charlene is hungry, she makes a sandwich.

2. The guitar was less expensive at Melody Music Shop.

3. Parker's birthday is January 27.

4. The Tour de France is a bicycle race through France.

5. Let's meet at the movie theater on Monday.

6. A squirrel raced through the trees in Highland Park.

7. My apartment is on the third floor.

8. Louise asked the banker for a loan.

9. The Statue of Liberty is in New York City.

10. Please take the garbage out.

Grammar Minutes · Grade 5 © 2009 Creative Teaching Press

Minute 24

Name _____

For Numbers 1–5, read the paragraph and circle the five plural nouns. Write them on the lines.

The climbers set off to reach the summit of Mt. Kilimanjaro. They carried knives, cooking utensils, and food with them. It would take a long time to reach the top and set up camp. They had been training for months with people around the area. What victory it would be to finally reach their destination!

1. _____

2. _____

3. _____

4. _____

5. _____

For Numbers 6–10, write the plural form for each noun.

6. beetle _____

7. hobby _____

8. mouse _____

9. half _____

10. echo _____

Plural Nouns Review

Minute 25

Name _____

For Numbers 1–5, rewrite each phrase in possessive form.

1. The department for men

_____

2. The bookshelf belonging to Cindy

_____

3. The windows of the galleries

_____

4. The crayons belonging to the kindergartner

_____

5. The water bottles belonging to the runners

_____

For Numbers 6–10, underline the singular possessive phrase and circle the plural possessive phrase in each sentence.

6. Melissa's motorcycle ran more smoothly than her friends' motorcycles.

7. The Dolphins' victory made Dad's day.

8. The flowers' pollen affected Jessica's allergies.

9. I don't like to walk to Daria's Grocery Store because of the neighborhood dogs' loud barking as I enter their territory.

10. Lisa's pet hamster can't climb onto the sofas' slippery cushions.

Grammar Minutes · Grade 5 © 2009 Creative Teaching Press

Minute 26

Name _____

For Numbers 1–5, circle the correct object pronoun(s) to complete each sentence.

1. Mom made lasagna for my brother and (me/I).

2. Mrs. Green chose Warren and (she/her) to finish the math problems on the board.

3. The puppy followed (they/them) home from the park.

4. The calculators belong to (she/her) and (he/him).

5. Lisa asked (he/him) and (I/me) to go to the movies.

For Numbers 6–10, write a subject pronoun to replace the underlined word or words in each sentence.

6. Ronald appears in many television commercials. _____

7. The turtle sunned itself on the rocks. _____

8. Air pollution is hazardous to the earth and to humans' health. _____

9. The twins will receive an award for their volunteer work at the daycare center. _____

10. Erin and I earn money by mowing our neighbors' lawns. _____

Subject and Object Pronouns Review

Minute 27

Name _____

For Numbers 1–5, write the correct possessive pronoun to complete each sentence.

1. When Jenna's baby brother laughs, _____ new baby teeth show.

2. _____ neighbor's house has lights that turn off automatically.

3. Trent and Carla are working on _____ project.

4. Even though Liz said she wasn't good at bowling, I found out _____ top score in bowling is 219.

5. We could hardly believe _____ eyes.

For Numbers 6–10, write the correct reflexive pronoun from the box to complete each sentence.

| themselves | herself | himself | itself | yourself |

6. Henry built a clubhouse all by _____.

7. Kenlyn ate a hot dog, but Sarah made a salad for _____.

8. He and his friends bought concert tickets for _____.

9. You should drive to the store by _____.

10. A lizard can grow _____ a new tail.

Grammar Minutes · Grade 5 © 2009 Creative Teaching Press

Minute 28

Name _____

For Numbers 1–5, circle the correct relative pronoun to complete each sentence.

1. Mother Teresa was a woman (who/that) served the poor her entire life.

2. The antique chair (who/that) belongs to my mother is a family heirloom.

3. Belinda has a favorite hat (who/that) once belonged to her sister.

4. The television (who/that) has loud speakers is better for playing video games.

5. The person in the drama club (who/that) raises the most money for the trip will win a prize.

For Numbers 6–10, write *Yes* if the indefinite pronoun in the phrase is used correctly. Write *No* if it is not.

6. Many of the students put <u>his backpacks</u> under the desks. _____

7. <u>Either boy</u> can drive his truck. _____

8. Someone brought <u>their skateboard</u> into the house. _____

9. Does everyone have <u>their homework</u> finished? _____

10. Both of the boys received telescopes for <u>their birthdays</u>. _____

Relative and Indefinite Pronouns Review

Minute 29

Name _____

Underline the action verb in each sentence. Write another action verb on the line to replace the one you underlined.

1. The glider soars through the air.   _____

2. Evan drives over the Rocky Mountains.   _____

3. The stars sparkle in the night sky.   _____

4. The lamb leaps across the meadow.   _____

5. Marcy and Mike skate to the park.   _____

6. The farmer cuts the corn.   _____

7. The storm is here, and I lost my umbrella.   _____

8. The boat sails into the harbor.   _____

9. The diver is not afraid as he swims.   _____

10. Helen is happy because she hit a home run.   _____

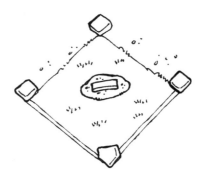

Grammar Minutes · Grade 5 © 2009 Creative Teaching Press

Minute 30

Name _____

For Numbers 1–5, underline the linking verb in each sentence.
(**Hint**: A *linking verb* does not express action. It connects the subject to the rest of the information about the subject.)

1. That octopus is large and scary.

2. I am sleepy after my long trip.

3. Apples are my favorite fruit.

4. The animals in the zoo are interesting to watch.

5. The airplanes were all late because of the storm.

For Numbers 6–10, circle the sentence in each pair that has a helping verb.
(**Hint**: A *helping verb* is the first word of a verb phrase and often sets the time and mood.)

6. a. She will go to the movies with Brenda.

    b. She watched the movie with Brenda.

7. a. Janice and Nicolas helped their mother with the cooking.

    b. Janice and Nicolas are helping their mother cook.

8. a. We meet to play soccer on Wednesday.

    b. We have been playing soccer for an hour.

9. a. She is nice.

    b. She is acting nice.

10. a. I am going to my house.

    b. I want to go home.

Grammar Minutes · Grade 5 © 2009 Creative Teaching Press

Linking and Helping Verbs

Minute 31

Name _____

Write the past tense forms of each verb below.
(**Hint:** Not all past tense verbs end in –*ed.*)

Present Tense	Past Tense
1. sail	_____
2. scream	_____
3. fly	_____
4. answer	_____
5. grow	_____
6. act	_____
7. wear	_____
8. write	_____
9. boil	_____
10. break	_____

Grammar Minutes · Grade 5 © 2009 Creative Teaching Press

Minute 32

Name _____

Add **–ed** or **–ing** to the verb to correctly complete each sentence.

1. Who _____ the Internet?

invent

2. The lionesses _____ in the cool hours of the evening.

hunt

3. Travis was _____ about his bicycle tricks.

joke

4. Mrs. Jones _____ there would be a math test on Thursday.

mention

5. Thousands of people are _____ to warmer locations.

move

6. The sporting goods store is _____ a discount for frequent shoppers.

offer

7. The queen _____ the country for more than 40 years.

rule

8. Shelly is _____ a surprise birthday party for her mother.

plan

9. The workers are _____ the produce for the restaurant.

unload

10. Aunt Betsy is _____ from Vermont for a week.

visit

Grammar Minutes · Grade 5 © 2009 Creative Teaching Press

More Present and Past Tense Verbs

Minute 33

Name _____

For Numbers 1–5, circle the correct verb to complete each sentence.
(**Hint:** The verbs *lay, set,* and *raise* are used with a direct object.)

1. Please (lay/lie) the books on the table.

2. Robert (lies/lays) on the couch because he isn't feeling well.

3. Mr. Henderson (set/sit) the microscopes on the tables.

4. We taught our dog to (sit/set) on command.

5. The hills (rise/raise) above the valley.

For Numbers 6–10, write the correct past tense verb on the line.

6. Ms. Fortunato_____ the curtain and the show began.
   raised   rose

7. Yesterday the cat _____ in the sunshine on the porch.
   lay   laid

8. Cherise _____ the plates around the table.
   past   passed

9. We each _____ at a computer station in the library.
   sat   set

10. I always _____ my library card right on the counter.
   lay   lie

Grammar Minutes · Grade 5 © 2009 Creative Teaching Press

Minute 34

Name _____

For Numbers 1–5, write the correct form of the verb to complete each phrase.

Example: Wait

I wait

You wait

He waits

They wait

1. Laugh

I _____

You _____

She _____

They _____

2. Ask

I _____

You _____

He _____

They _____

3. Start

I _____

You _____

It _____

They _____

4. Paint

I _____

You _____

He _____

They _____

5. Dance

I _____

You _____

She _____

They _____

For Numbers 6–10, circle the correct verb form to complete each sentence.

6. Jerry and June (mops/mop) the floor.

7. The fifth-grade class (plant/plants) a tree every year.

8. The bee (stings/sting) the predator who threatens it.

9. He (turn/turns) off the light when leaving the room.

10. Fran (ignore/ignores) the telephone while she is studying.

Subject and Verb Agreement

Minute 35

Name _____

Circle the correct verb form to complete each sentence.

1. Our baseball team (is/are) the best in the state.

2. The class (earn/earns) a quarter for each bake sale item sold.

3. The number of people who like Brussels sprouts (is/are) very small.

4. The hills (is/are) gleaming with white snow.

5. Doctors (is/are) very caring people.

6. Chandra's glasses (is/are) on her desk.

7. Raven and Jan (is/are) playing tetherball.

8. Either William's brother or my mom (drive/drives) us to school.

9. Neither Chris nor James will (wear/wears) braces anymore.

10. The scissors (is/are) in the top drawer.

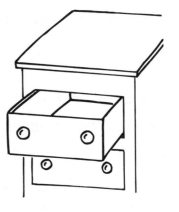

Minute 36

Name _____

For Numbers 1–5, either circle the action verb or underline the linking verb in each sentence.

1. The roller coaster raced around the track.

2. A snowman melts in the sunshine.

3. Natalie was fourteen years old.

4. Pete and Hank built a go-cart from scraps of wood.

5. He is very tired.

For Numbers 6–10, write a sentence that includes an action verb.

6. It is snowy outside.

The snow _____

7. It is nice weather in the city today.

The sun _____

8. My friend and I had fun at the concert.

My friend and I _____

9. Lisa is tired.

Lisa _____

10. I am hungry.

My stomach _____

Grammar Minutes · Grade 5 © 2009 Creative Teaching Press

Action and Linking Verbs Review

Minute 37

Name _____

Write *H* if the verb in the sentence helps another verb or expresses time or mood. Write *L* if the verb links two ideas together.

1. I will run to the store quickly. _____

2. The capital of the United States is Washington, D.C. _____

3. The peaches are ripe. _____

4. The bananas will ripen if you store them in a paper bag. _____

5. They should walk to the store rather than drive. _____

6. He is taking his time. _____

7. The shoes were in the closet. _____

8. He can store his shoes in the closet. _____

9. The evening sky is beautiful. _____

10. The chef seems capable. _____

Grammar Minutes · Grade 5 © 2009 Creative Teaching Press

Minute 38

Name _____

For Numbers 1–5, write the past tense form of each verb.

1. run _____

4. walk _____

2. dive _____

5. think _____

3. freeze _____

For Numbers 6–10, add *–ing* or *–ed* to the verb to correctly complete each sentence.

6. Janice is _____ the crumbs that fell on the floor.
sweep

7. When the glue has _____, we can take home our projects.
dry

8. The drummers are _____ in a parade this Saturday.
march

9. All of the athletes _____ after completing the race.
stretch

10. The fireworks _____ in the sky.
explode

Present and Past Tense Verbs Review

Minute 39

Name _____

For Numbers 1–5, circle the correct verb to complete each sentence.

1. Where did you (lay/lie) the pencils?

2. It feels good to (lie/lay) down after a long bike ride.

3. Jimmy likes to (set/sit) out all his materials before he paints.

4. Mom honked the car horn as we (passed/past) the school.

5. The class will (rise/raise) money to take a field trip.

For Numbers 6–10, write *Yes* if the correct verb is used for each sentence. Write *No* if it is not.

6. We <u>passed</u> time by playing road trip games.   _____

7. The bread <u>will raise</u> to the top of the pan.   _____

8. I <u>lie</u> the presents on the table.   _____

9. The vase <u>sits</u> on the mantle in our living room.   _____

10. After you're finished reading the newspaper, <u>sit</u> it on the shelf.   _____

Grammar Minutes · Grade 5 © 2009 Creative Teaching Press

Minute 40

Name _____

Circle the correct verb form to complete each sentence.

1. Candice (expect/expects) her team to win the competition.

2. The tired old dog (flop/flops) down on the kitchen floor.

3. There (was/were) too many students standing in the hallway.

4. In my grandfather's attic (is/are) dozens of old cameras.

5. Blanca, my older sister, (plan/plans) to attend Stanford University in the fall.

6. The flesh of the fruit (is/are) tender and juicy.

7. Harry (wish/wishes) his best friend would get well soon.

8. The teacher (eat/eats) lunch in the school cafeteria along with his students.

9. Among the top three tennis players in the world (is/are) two Europeans and one Canadian.

10. The adventurous climber (use/uses) ropes and other safety devices as she climbs the face of the cliff.

Minute 41

Name _____

For Numbers 1–5, circle the descriptive adjective(s) in each sentence.

1. The awkward foal returned to the barn.

2. The magic carpet flew over the city.

3. The baker delivered delicious cookies for the teachers' meeting.

4. A tiny, black puppy romped in the white snow.

5. The dirty, smelly shoes were left on the step.

For Numbers 6–10, use an adjective from the box to best complete each sentence. Use each adjective only once.

demanding	little	green
beautiful	unpredictable	mashed

6. The _____ volcano finally erupted last week.

7. Ginny is saving her money to buy a _____ necklace.

8. The _____ passenger asked the driver to listen to his directions.

9. Kevin's _____ brother likes _____ balloons.

10. The cafeteria is serving _____ potatoes for lunch today.

Grammar Minutes · Grade 5 © 2009 Creative Teaching Press

Minute 42

Name _____

Replace the underlined word in each sentence with a descriptive adjective from the box that means about the same thing.

narrow	generously	dangerous	exquisite
speedy	plump	hilariously	contented
level	humble	helpful	immense
diamond	playful	unintelligent	kind

1. The <u>nice</u> boy picked up the fallen books. _____

2. The <u>bad</u> snake chased a rat. _____

3. She looked at the <u>pretty</u> jewels in the glass case. _____

4. The <u>fast</u> car raced along the highway. _____

5. A <u>fat</u> cow slowly chewed hay. _____

6. The <u>happy</u> girl ate an apple as she waited for her friend. _____

7. The <u>flat</u> road stretched as far as we could see. _____

8. Alex is a <u>good</u> friend who always listens. _____

9. The <u>big</u> umbrella kept me dry. _____

10. A <u>funny</u> seal played in the water. _____

Grammar Minutes · Grade 5 © 2009 Creative Teaching Press

More Adjectives

Minute 43

Name _____

Circle the correct form of the adjective.
(**Hint**: Generally, add *–er* to most one-syllable adjectives to show comparison. Use *more* for adjectives with two- or more syllables.)

1. smoother   more smooth

2. fresher   more fresh

3. generaler   more general

4. difficulter   more difficult

5. jealouser   more jealous

6. kinder   more kind

7. lighter   more light

8   memorabler   more memorable

9. quicker   more quick

10. helplesser   more helpless

Grammar Minutes · Grade 5 © 2009 Creative Teaching Press

Minute 44

Name _____

For Numbers 1–5, circle the correct adjective to complete each sentence.

1. Mint chocolate chip is the (good/best) ice cream flavor available.

2. A broken leg is (worse/more bad) than a broken fingernail.

3. Sharice picked (most/more) berries than Frank.

4. That movie was (less/least) exciting than the one we saw last week.

5. The sour pickles were (more worse/worse) than the lemons.

For Numbers 6–10, write the comparative and superlative form of each adjective.

Adjective	Comparative	Superlative
Ex. high	higher	highest
6. flat		
7. brave		
8. strong		
9. calm		
10. lean		

Grammar Minutes · Grade 5 © 2009 Creative Teaching Press

Comparative and Superlative Adjectives

Minute 45

Name _____

For Numbers 1–5, circle the adverb in each sentence.
(**Hint**: An *adverb* is a word that tells *how, when,* or *where* something happens.)

1. The Bulldogs played mightily but lost the soccer game.

2. The boulder landed heavily on the valley floor.

3. Trisha waited eagerly while her mother paid for the new dress.

4. Measure exactly how long the shelf should be.

5. The spinning top twirled crazily before falling off the table.

For Numbers 6–10, circle the correct use of *good* or *well* in each sentence.
(**Hint**: Use *good* as an adjective. Example: She is having a good day. Use *well* as an adverb. Example: She draws well.)

6. The chocolate cupcakes smell (good/well).

7. Kate played (good/well) in the game.

8. The knots in the line look (good/well).

9. Nadia danced (good/well) at her ballet recital.

10. Hee Jin did (good/well) on her science test.

Grammar Minutes · Grade 5 © 2009 Creative Teaching Press

Minute 46

Name _____

Write *how, when, where, how often,* or *to what degree* to tell what the underlined adverb describes.

1. The students worked <u>quickly</u>. _____

2. Drake visits his grandmother <u>frequently</u>. _____

3. Mr. Rodriguez finds teaching <u>extremely</u> enjoyable. _____

4. Grace will enter middle school <u>next</u> year. _____

5. You left your lunch <u>there</u> on the table. _____

6. I am leaving <u>today</u> for summer camp. _____

7. Julie worked <u>carefully</u> on her egg painting. _____

8. The doctor pressed <u>gently</u> on Sara's broken arm. _____

9. Ms. Muldoon checks our homework <u>daily</u>. _____

10. Josh was <u>very</u> grateful when his wallet was found. _____

More Adverbs

Minute 47

Name _____

For Numbers 1–10, write the comparative and superlative form of each adverb.
(Hint: Use either *-er* and *-est* or *more* and *most*)

Adverb	Comparative	Superlative
1. fast	_____	_____
2. quietly	_____	_____
3. early	_____	_____
4. often	_____	_____
5. slowly	_____	_____
6. far	_____	_____
7. near	_____	_____
8. carefully	_____	_____
9. soon	_____	_____
10. gracefully	_____	_____

Minute 48

Name _____

For Numbers 1–5, circle the correct form of the adjective to complete each sentence.
(**Hint**: Adjectives that end in *-er* compare two things, and adjectives that end in *–est* compare more than two things.)

1. Mrs. Klein's math class is (more hard/harder) than Mr. Brown's.

2. My scoop of ice cream is (larger/largest) than Tommy's.

3. The drum is (more louder/louder) than the guitar.

4. Danielle is the (more smaller/smallest) of the triplets.

5. Of all the students in the class, Gabriel is the (most tallest/tallest).

For Numbers 6–10, write the comparative or superlative form of each adjective.

	Adjective	Comparative	Superlative
6.	good	better	_____
7.	bad	_____	worst
8.	little	less	_____
9.	few	_____	fewest
10.	much	more	_____

Adjectives Review

Minute 49

Name _____

Circle the word that the underlined adverb modifies.
(**Hint:** An *adverb* can modify a verb, an adjective, or another adverb.)

1. We <u>hesitantly</u> ate the okra Mom served us.

2. The mother chimpanzee held her baby <u>snugly</u> against her chest.

3. We <u>often</u> go to the swimming pool at the community center.

4. Contests are held <u>locally</u> for anyone who is interested.

5. Javier <u>thoughtfully</u> considered his options before deciding.

6. The strangely shaped teddy bear sat <u>awkwardly</u> on the shelf in the toy store.

7. The guests spoke <u>loudly</u> in the dining room.

8. Sasha marched <u>purposefully</u> to the teacher's desk.

9. Mrs. Westland is <u>very</u> generous.

10. I will remember this vacation <u>forever</u>.

Grammar Minutes · Grade 5 © 2009 Creative Teaching Press

Minute 50

Name _____

Write *adj* if the word underlined is an adjective or *adv* if the word underlined is an adverb.

1. Runs <u>quickly</u> _____

2. <u>Playful</u> puppy _____

3. Gaze <u>longingly</u> _____

4. <u>Cold</u> water _____

5. Eat <u>frequently</u> _____

6. Speak <u>quietly</u> _____

7. <u>Quiet</u> students _____

8. <u>Fried</u> chicken _____

9. <u>Hard</u> rock _____

10. <u>Hardly</u> working _____

Adjectives and Adverbs

Minute 51

Name _____

Circle the word(s) the underlined adjective or adverb modifies.

1. The brilliant blue chair is the <u>most uncomfortable</u> seat in the room.

2. The moon shone <u>brightly</u> over the majestic mountains.

3. We had an <u>incredible</u> view from the window of our cabin.

4. The drum beat a <u>contagious</u> rhythm.

5. Mom says the washing machine runs <u>constantly</u>.

6. There were <u>subtle</u> signs Ernie was planning a party.

7. Wendy <u>effortlessly</u> climbed the rock wall.

8. The player bounced the ball <u>repeatedly</u> before taking a shot.

9. Our group worked <u>hard</u> on the science fair project.

10. Zack is the <u>most experienced</u> traveler in the group.

Grammar Minutes · Grade 5 © 2009 Creative Teaching Press

Minute 52

Name _____

For Numbers 1–5, circle the two prepositions in each sentence.
(**Hint**: A *preposition* shows a relationship of a noun or pronoun to another word in the sentence and often tells where, what kind, when, or how. Example: I ran *along* the shore.)

1. Roland had to choose between the bearded dragon and the green iguana as his pet.

2. The paleontologist with the white gloves placed the fossil inside the heavy glass case.

3. The two girls looked at each other across the table.

4. Our football team celebrated at a restaurant after winning the championship game.

5. The willow tree beside the brook up the road is my favorite place to read.

For Numbers 6–10, use a preposition from the box to correctly complete each sentence. Use each preposition only once.

inside	beneath	with	since	near

6. The students put their lunch boxes _____ their lockers.

7. The cave _____ the mouth of the river was full of bats.

8. Lava forms well _____ the earth's surface.

9. The little boat _____ a striped sail won the race.

10. _____ she discovered stamp collecting, Sara has given up gardening.

Prepositions

Minute 53

Name _____

For Numbers 1–5, write *between* or *among* to correctly complete each sentence.
(**Hint**: Use *between* when you are referring to two people, items, or ideas; use *among* when referring to three or more.)

1. The contest is _____ Shana and Wren.

2. Who _____ you is the greatest warrior?

3. I had to choose _____ chocolate chip and vanilla ice cream.

4. Isabella finished her homework _____ seven and eight o'clock.

5. Voters will decide _____ the Democrats and the Republicans.

For Numbers 6–10, write *Yes* if the correct preposition is used. Write *No* if it is not.

6. How many states are <u>among</u> California and Texas? _____

7. Quan, Fran, and David are <u>among</u> the favorites to win the golf tournament. _____

8. Mrs. Sanger will choose <u>among</u> the Mighty Mongrels and the Laughing Labradors for the winner of the talent show. _____

9. My coach is the woman standing <u>between</u> the two men in red jackets. _____

10. Choosing a book <u>between</u> so many great titles is difficult. _____

Grammar Minutes · Grade 5 © 2009 Creative Teaching Press

Minute 54

Name _____

Circle either *a* or *b* to show which underlined phrase is the prepositional phrase in each sentence.
(**Hint:** *A prepositional phrase* begins with a preposition and ends with a noun.)

1. <u>In Australia,</u> kangaroos <u>can be found</u> roaming in the wild.
       a   b

2. The school <u>counselor encouraged</u> us to think <u>about our future career choices.</u>
                       a   b

3. Jimmy <u>had trained</u> <u>for the X Games</u> in snowboarding.
             a   b

4. Benjamin Franklin had <u>many accomplishments</u> <u>as a great American leader.</u>
                            a   b

5. <u>In 1958,</u> the United States launched <u>its first successful satellite,</u> *Explorer 1.*
      a   b

6. <u>Now happy,</u> Carla skipped off <u>with her best friend, Janelle.</u>
       a   b

7. <u>In live concert,</u> Ian's favorite band was <u>even better.</u>
        a   b

8. Pluto takes more than 247 years <u>to revolve</u> <u>around the sun.</u>
                               a   b

9. Tropical rain forests have <u>the greatest variety</u> of plant species <u>on earth.</u>
                          a   b

10. Nigel and Jack decided <u>to cook</u> macaroni and cheese <u>for lunch.</u>
                         a   b

Prepositional Phrases

Minute 55

Name _____

For Numbers 1–5, use at least one prepositional phrase found in the box to write a sentence.

about four o'clock	across the street	in my space
against the wall	along the path	of the crowd
around the bend	behind the door	over the hill

1. _____

2. _____

3. _____

4. _____

5. _____

For Number 6–10, circle the prepositional phrase in each sentence.

6. She put the present inside the box and mailed it.

7. "Please put all papers on my desk," said Mrs. Larmer.

8. She could barely see through the window.

9. Will you go to the party or will you go home?

10. Sarah walked on the sidewalk, facing traffic.

Minute 56

Name _____

For Numbers 1–5, write the article *a* or *an* to correctly complete each phrase.
(**Hint**: Use *a* before a word that begins with a consonant sound. Use *an* before a word that begins with a vowel sound.)

1. _____ fox and her babies

2. _____ orange and a banana

3. _____ honest answer

4. _____ busy city

5. _____ ancient scroll

For Numbers 6–10, write the article(s) that best completes each sentence.
(Use *a, an,* or *the*.)

6. Melanie's team, the Stingrays, just scored three goals to win _____ championship hockey game.

7. They played in _____ championship tournament all week and had to beat _____ good team to make it to the finals.

8. _____ game was held on Sunday, March 9, 2008, at Madison Square Garden in New York City.

9. Billy saw _____ opportunity to score in the last minutes of _____ second period and succeeded.

10. It was _____ great victory and _____ honor to be declared the best team in the country.

Grammar Minutes · Grade 5 © 2009 Creative Teaching Press

Articles

Minute 57

Name _____

For Numbers 1–5, circle the correct conjunction to complete the sentence.
(**Hint**: A *conjunction* is a word that joins words or groups of words. It can show togetherness or contrast. Example: Patricia *and* Mark went to the restaurant, *but* Mark did not eat.)

1. The rain began, (yet/since/so) the ceremony was moved inside.

2. Albania is a small country, (and/since/or) it is one of Europe's poorest.

3. Sound travels fast. (Since/However/So), light travels faster.

4. Sidney Crosby was born in Dartmouth, Nova Scotia, (so/although/but) grew up in Cole Harbour.

5. Ancient Sumerians developed cuneiform, (and/or/since) Ancient Egyptians developed hieroglyphics.

For Numbers 6–10, write a conjunction from the box to best complete each sentence. Do not use a conjunction more than once.

and	yet	so	but	since	or	although	because

6. The new house was complete, _____ it had no furniture.

7. Patty _____ Pricilla are sisters.

8. The cafeteria served hamburgers _____ not hot dogs.

9. My friend asked if I wanted to see either a comedy _____ an action movie.

10. _____ the clown was somewhat funny, he also annoyed me.

Grammar Minutes · Grade 5 © 2009 Creative Teaching Press

Minute 58

Name _____

For Numbers 1–4, rewrite the two sentences as a single sentence. Use a conjunction to join them.
(**Hint:** Eliminate words that repeat, and then combine the rest of the words to shorten sentences and save time.)

1. I will go to the park. I will get Jerome.

_____

2. Veronica enjoys ballet. She doesn't like ballet recitals.

_____

3. The guitarist played a quiet ballad. The singer hummed softly.

_____

4. The Internet is a good source of information. The Internet also provides entertainment.

_____

For Numbers 5–10, write *Yes* if the example is a compound sentence. Write *No* if it is not.

5. Ponce de Leon explored the southeast coast of North America. _____

6. I will take a weight training class and an aerobics class. _____

7. He and I will take a trip down to San Francisco in the fall or winter. _____

8. Alexander Graham Bell invented the telephone. _____

9. The teachers were ready for the start of school, but the students were not ready for summer to end. _____

10. Icicles hung from the trees, and children made snowmen in the yard. _____

Grammar Minutes • Grade 5 © 2009 Creative Teaching Press

Compound Sentences

Minute 59

Name _____

For Numbers 1–5, underline the appositive in each sentence. Circle the noun or pronoun that it describes.
(Hint: An *appositive* identifies or renames the words before it. Example: Our teachers, *Mr. Jones and Ms. Liddell,* went to a conference on Friday.)

1. Jake, the soccer star, is the most popular boy in school.

2. Dr. Williams, my pediatrician, checked my reflexes with a small rubber hammer.

3. Our class finished reading <u>Charlie and the Chocolate Factory</u>, Roald Dahl's masterpiece, last week.

4. Is that your sister, Hannah, with the ponytail?

5. The Indianapolis 500 race, the epitome of American racing, was first held in 1911.

For Numbers 6–10, write *D* if the underlined portion is a dependent clause. Write *I* if the underlined portion is an independent clause.
(Hint: A *dependent clause* does not express a complete thought and is not a complete sentence on its own. An *independent clause* expresses a complete thought and could stand alone as its own sentence.)

6. Come to my house, and <u>we will start on our science project.</u> _____

7. All stations will televise the president's speech <u>when he speaks.</u> _____

8. My brother will drive us to the movies <u>after he is finished with work.</u> _____

9. The professor announced an exam, and <u>students scrambled to study.</u> _____

10. Troy will enter the yodeling contest <u>if Maggie enters.</u> _____

Grammar Minutes · Grade 5 © 2009 Creative Teaching Press

Minute 60

Name _____

Underline the prepositional phrase(s) in each sentence.
(**Hint**: The remaining words should still make a complete sentence.)

1. The entire class went to the performance except Charles.

2. Sailors use the stars to find their location on earth.

3. Groovy girls in the 1960s wore their hair very long and very straight.

4. Christopher Columbus landed in the Bahamas.

5. New Year's Day is a big celebration for our family.

6. Many companies in our community allow employees time off to vote.

7. Percussion instruments make sound when they are struck by the musician.

8. She closed the book and walked out of the library into the bright sunshine.

9. Nate grew up on a farm in West Virginia.

10. The United Nations was founded in 1945, after World War II ended.

Prepositions Review

Minute 61

Name _____

For Numbers 1–5, write the article *a* or *an* to correctly complete each phrase.

1. _____ kneepad

2. _____ high-flying kite

3. _____ biology class

4. _____ hour

5. _____ once-in-a-lifetime opportunity

For Numbers 6–10, circle the article that correctly completes each sentence.

6. Jefferson Elementary School held three fundraisers to buy new computers for (the/an) technology lab.

7. If you have any questions about (an/a) problem on the math homework, please write which problem number it is in your journal.

8. Preston displayed (an/the) coin he found at an old ghost town.

9. (An/A) G-rated movie is appropriate for all ages.

10. Janet wore (a/an) orange dress with flowers on the sleeve.

Grammar Minutes · Grade 5 © 2009 Creative Teaching Press

Minute 62

Name _____

For Numbers 1–5, circle the conjunction that correctly completes each sentence.

1. I say I'm busy, (yet/and/or) I always find myself saying yes when people ask for help.

2. I turn my ringer off at night (because/however/yet) I don't want to be disturbed.

3. The phone not only woke me up (and/yet/but also) woke up my sister.

4. Bring either a pen (but also/yet/or) a pencil.

5. I bought a new skirt (however/and/but also) a new sweater.

For Numbers 6–10, circle the conjunctions that join two or more things. Underline the conjunctions that contrast two or more things (or that change the direction of the sentence).

6. We looked at the take-out menus and circled our food choices.

7. We always order fried rice, so this time we tried something different.

8. Do you want noodles or stir-fry?

9. Gemma likes soy sauce and pepper on all of her food.

10. Daniel eats a lot, although he always regrets it later.

Grammar Minutes • Grade 5 © 2009 Creative Teaching Press

Minute 63

Name _____

For Numbers 1–6, write *Yes* if the example is a compound sentence. Write *No* if is not.

1. Valerie will visit Ireland to view the Book of Kells , but she will not have time to tour the countryside. _____

2. Janet cut the cake, and we all sang "Happy Birthday." _____

3. Jay and Luis felt upset when their soccer team lost. _____

4. Air pollution is harmful to plants and to animals. _____

5. Jennifer will join the chorus, and she will also take piano lessons this year. _____

6. Chinese Americans and Korean Americans often celebrate the lunar New Year. _____

For Numbers 7–10, rewrite the sentences as a single sentence.

7. At summer's end, many students pack up for college. They drive to their campuses.

   _____

8. The pizza was cut into eight pieces. It was all gone shortly thereafter.

   _____

9. The athletes in the triathlon run. The athletes also bike for miles. They also have to swim.

   _____

10. I know how to ride a bicycle. I also can ride a unicycle. My friend knows how to ride a bicycle and unicycle too.

    _____

Grammar Minutes · Grade 5 © 2009 Creative Teaching Press

Minute 64

Name _____

For Numbers 1–5, write a sentence using each of the appositives below.

my favorite book	a movie released last week
my hardest subject in school	the tiny kitten
my sister's friend	

1. _____

2. _____

3. _____

4. _____

5. _____

For Numbers 6–10, write *D* if the underlined portion is a dependent clause. Write *I* if the underlined portion is an independent clause.

6. My little sister goes to the preschool <u>where Miss Wendy works.</u> _____

7. Patrick earned fourteen dollars by mowing lawns, and <u>he planned to spend it on video games.</u> _____

8. It was impossible to ignore <u>the terrible stench that came from the hallway.</u> _____

9. The tree is withering and <u>losing its leaves already.</u> _____

10. Brianna walked to Nancy's house, and <u>together they went to the mall.</u> _____

Minute 65

Name _____

Add another word to the beginning or the end of each word below to create a compound word.

1. air   _____

2. back   _____

3. brain   _____

4. day   _____

5. dog   _____

6. heart   _____

7. counter   _____

8. down   _____

9. earth   _____

10. man   _____

Grammar Minutes · Grade 5 © 2009 Creative Teaching Press

Minute 66

Name _____

Write a synonym for each underlined word.

1. The <u>loud</u> blast from the car horn shook him awake. _____

2. Jack refused to be <u>afraid</u> of a tiny spider. _____

3. You are out if you step outside the <u>boundary</u>. _____

4. Dr. Garrison was very <u>concerned</u> about Amber's high fever. _____

5. The <u>level</u> of the water continued to rise. _____

6. After baseball practice, my uniform is <u>dirty</u>. _____

7. The sunset was <u>pretty</u>. _____

8. A <u>bright</u> light filled the auditorium and the show began. _____

9. The cornfields seem to go on <u>forever</u>. _____

10. It is best to fly a kite on a <u>windy</u> day. _____

Synonyms

Minute 67

Name _____

Write a synonym for each word.

1. smart   _____

2. narrow   _____

3. apart   _____

4. argue   _____

5. center   _____

6. awful   _____

7. shy   _____

8. smelly   _____

9. cute   _____

10. path   _____

Minute 68

Name _____

Draw a line to match each word with its antonym.

1. part •		• ancient
2. praise •		• whole
3. modern •		• slow
4. ceiling •		• rough
5. speedy •		• criticize
6. protected •		• subtract
7. add •		• intermittent
8. constant •		• unsheltered
9. asleep •		• floor
10. smooth •		• awake

Grammar Minutes · Grade 5 © 2009 Creative Teaching Press

Antonyms

Minute 69

Name _____

Write an antonym for each word.

1. tardy   _____

2. new   _____

3. rotten   _____

4. scarce   _____

5. flat   _____

6. locked   _____

7. sink   _____

8. lazy   _____

9. empty   _____

10. dishonest   _____

Grammar Minutes · Grade 5 © 2009 Creative Teaching Press

Minute 70

Name _____

For each sentence below, use the other form of the underlined homograph to write a new sentence.

(**Hint**: *Homographs* are words that are spelled the same, but have different meanings and often have different pronunciations.)

1. <u>Close</u> the screen door to keep the mosquitoes out.

_____

2. Barry caught the biggest <u>bass</u> I've ever seen.

_____

3. We watched the <u>dove</u> hover over her babies.

_____

4. Where will we <u>house</u> the hamster?

_____

5. The snake prefers to eat <u>live</u> mice.

_____

6. Mrs. Billings had to <u>separate</u> the two mischievous girls.

_____

7. The weather forecaster <u>projects</u> rain for the weekend.

_____

8. How can you mend a <u>tear</u> in the tent?

_____

9. What is your <u>address</u>?

_____

10. Johnny will <u>present</u> the award to Michelle.

_____

Grammar Minutes · Grade 5 © 2009 Creative Teaching Press

Homographs

Minute 71

Name _____

Write the correct homophone to complete each sentence.
(**Hint**: *Homophones* are words that sound the same but are spelled differently and have different meanings.)

1. Vera _____ seven cupcakes.
   ate   eight

2. What type of _____ do you like to have for breakfast?
   cereal   serial

3. We _____ Tony and Elaine talking about the birthday party.
   herd   heard

4. The _____ efficiently cleaned each room.
   maid   made

5. The actor studied her lines for the _____ of Juliet.
   roll   role

6. Our school's _____ wears a tie every day.
   principal   principle

7. The class gave a loud _____ when the teacher announced a quiz.
   groan   grown

8. The teacher's helper _____ around the papers.
   passed   past

9. I can't _____ to watch.
   bear   bare

10. The boat appeared out of the _____.
    mist   missed

Grammar Minutes · Grade 5 © 2009 Creative Teaching Press

Minute 72

Name _____

Circle the correct word in parentheses to complete each sentence.

1. Irena went (too/to) the museum.

2. Brad and I saw (two/too) elk walking through the woods.

3. Rene had chili for lunch, (to/too).

4. (Too/Two) many students packed into the bus.

5. (There/They're) are no seats left.

6. Mary and Kristine went to get (their/they're) backpacks.

7. (They're/Their) winning the game.

8. (It's/Its) Pilar's turn to play.

9. When (your/you're) finished with your dinner, please clear your plate.

10. The whale created a huge splash when it smacked (its/it's) fluke on the water.

Grammar Minutes · Grade 5 © 2009 Creative Teaching Press

More Homophones

Minute 73

Name _____

Write a synonym and an antonym for each word.

Word	Synonym	Antonym
1. tired	_____	_____
2. similar	_____	_____
3. noisy	_____	_____
4. receive	_____	_____
5. comical	_____	_____
6. increase	_____	_____
7. stroll	_____	_____
8. equal	_____	_____
9. valiant	_____	_____
10. grief	_____	_____

Grammar Minutes · Grade 5 © 2009 Creative Teaching Press

Minute 74

Name _____

For Numbers 1–5, write the homograph to complete each sentence.
(**Hint:** The word is used in the sentence.)

1. Kylie will present Bridget with a _____.

2. The nurse wound the bandage around the _____.

3. We have one minute to find the _____ details.

4. The contract states Harvey must not _____ any
   contagious diseases.

5. Troops will not desert the army in the _____.

For Numbers 6–10, complete each sentence with a homophone from the box.

course/coarse	kernel/colonel	feet/feat
night/knight	allowed/aloud	

6. Deanne ran the _____ without tipping any hurdles.

7. Only one _____ was left in the popcorn popper.

8. It was an incredible _____ to climb the rock wall.

9. The _____ stormed the castle to save the damsel
   in distress.

10. Papa _____ me to use his fishing rod.

Homographs and Homophones Review

Minute 75

Name _____

Write *Yes* if the sentence is written correctly. Write *No* if it is not.
(**Hint**: Negative words include *never, no, nobody, not, nowhere,* as well as *barely, hardly, scarcely.*
They also include any contractions with the word *not.*)

1. I don't got no gum. _____

2. He won't want nothing to drink. _____

3. They have not had hardly anybody over to their house. _____

4. Stephanie don't never take the bus. _____

5. The gardener won't water the plants when it's night. _____

6. Mr. Hoff can't barely see anything without his glasses. _____

7. Please don't forget to sign your name. _____

8. Nowhere do they not take that kind of credit card. _____

9. The parents told the children that they wouldn't go to Disneyland on vacation. _____

10. Our dogs, Maple and Sunny, are nowhere to be found. _____

Grammar Minutes · Grade 5 © 2009 Creative Teaching Press

Minute 76

Name _____

For Numbers 1–5, write the two words that combine to make each contraction.

1. they've _____ _____

2. she'd _____ _____

3. I'm _____ _____

4. don't _____ _____

5. hadn't _____ _____

For Numbers 6–10, write the contraction for each set of underlined words.

6. <u>You will</u> become a major league player one day. _____

7. That shirt <u>does not</u> go with those pants. _____

8. <u>Let us</u> go to the library tomorrow. _____

9. <u>Who would</u> like to see a movie tonight? _____

10. Tory <u>will not</u> finish the race. _____

Contractions

Minute 77

Name _____

For Numbers 1–5, insert commas in the correct places.

1. Pedro please remember to buy milk butter and eggs.

2. Yes I would like French fries with my hamburger.

3. Marie Curie a Nobel Prize winner was a physical chemist.

4. Tornadoes can happen anytime but they are most common between March and July.

5. An insect's body is divided into the head thorax and abdomen.

For Numbers 6–10, write *Yes* if all necessary commas are included and in the correct place. Write *No* if they are not.

6. My aunt Earleen is moving to Austin, Texas. _____

7. "It's time for ballet class", declared Mom. _____

8. On May 6 1937, the Hindenburg burst into flames upon descent. _____

9. Noah quietly asked, "Who is the bus driver?" _____

10. The Statue of Liberty was dedicated on October 28, 1886. _____

Grammar Minutes · Grade 5 © 2009 Creative Teaching Press

Minute 78

Name _____

Cross out the unnecessary negative words. Write other words on the line to replace them if needed.

1. I don't have no plans for the weekend. _____

2. There isn't no peanut butter in the cupboard. _____

3. I can't hardly believe Shelly would dye her hair purple. _____

4. The water couldn't barely trickle through the thick reeds. _____

5. Hank can't never go to the park. _____

6. There is not hardly any water left in my canteen. _____

7. Why isn't nobody cleaning up the living room? _____

8. I didn't do nothing. _____

9. There isn't nothing to do during the long summer months. _____

10. We aren't never going to do nothing. _____

Negatives Review

Minute 79

Name _____

Insert commas to correctly complete each sentence.

1. Tony Hawk was born May 12 1968 in San Diego California.

2. Tokyo Japan is one of the world's most populous cities.

3. Jayden said "You make the best chocolate pudding in the world."

4. The National Baseball Hall of Fame is located in Cooperstown New York.

5. "I watched the funniest program on television" Michael said.

6. Until the bridge is completed we will have to cross at the intersection down the street.

7. The storm clouds began to gather and we ran for cover in the cellar.

8. Quinn will you please answer questions three four and five for us?

9. Keisha the tallest girl in the class balanced herself carefully on a chair and pinned the picture to the bulletin board.

10. My three favorite Olympic sports are swimming basketball and gymnastics.

Grammar Minutes · Grade 5 © 2009 Creative Teaching Press

Minute 80

Name _____

Add a prefix to change the meaning of each word, and write its new definition. Use each prefix in the box only once.

anti-	dis-	fore-	inter-	mis-
non-	over-	re-	sub-	trans-

	Root word	Definition	Word with Prefix	Definition
1.	profit	gain	_____profit	_____
2.	eat	consume	_____eat	_____
3.	sight	see	_____sight	_____
4.	handle	manage	_____handle	_____
5.	view	look at	_____view	_____
6.	septic	infection	_____septic	_____
7.	agree	think alike	_____agree	_____
8.	national	of a country	_____national	_____
9.	marine	water	_____marine	_____
10.	port	place	_____port	_____

Grammar Minutes · Grade 5 © 2009 Creative Teaching Press

Minute 81

Name _____

Use the definition to add a suffix to each root word. Use each suffix in the box only once.

-ment	-en	-or	-est	-ful
-ic	-less	-able	-ous	-y

	Root word	Word with suffix	Definition
1.	afford	_____	Can pay for
2.	courage	_____	Characterized by bravery
3.	hope	_____	Having much faith
4.	sharp	_____	Most pointed
5.	wood	_____	Rigid
6.	poet	_____	Showing characteristics of a poet
7.	act	_____	A person who acts
8.	move	_____	Act of moving
9.	help	_____	Unable to aid
10.	fruit	_____	Having the essence of fruit

Grammar Minutes · Grade 5 © 2009 Creative Teaching Press

Minute 82

Name _____

Draw a line from the Greek or Latin root to its meaning. Draw another line from the meaning to the sample word.

Root	Meaning	Sample Word
1. dent •	• hear •	• graphic
2. aud •	• see •	• dentures
3. bio •	• trust •	• microscope
4. cred •	• take •	• biology
5. circ •	• tooth •	• vocal
6. graph •	• writing •	• circulate
7. prim •	• call •	• audio
8. voc •	• life •	• primary
9. cap •	• around •	• capture
10. scope •	• first •	• credible

Grammar Minutes · Grade 5 © 2009 Creative Teaching Press

Minute 83

Name _____

For Numbers 1–5, underline the Greek or Latin root(s) in each word.

1. dentist

2. biochemistry

3. circular

4. auditorium

5. telescope

For Numbers 6–10, circle the prefix and/or suffix in each word.

6. antibiotic

7. manageable

8. submerge

9. homeless

10. enjoyment

Grammar Minutes · Grade 5 © 2009 Creative Teaching Press

Minute 84

Name _____

For Numbers 1–4, underline the complete subject and circle the complete predicate in each sentence.

1. Babies cry.

2. The swimmers raced to the finish line.

3. The city of Los Angeles hosted the 1984 Olympic Games.

4. A rusty old car sat abandoned on the side of the road.

For Numbers 5–7, write *Yes* if the group of words is a complete sentence. Write *No* if it is not.

5. A cool glass of water. _____

6. Soccer practice is every Monday and Wednesday. _____

7. In the morning, after the sun has risen. _____

For Numbers 8–10, insert the correct punctuation at the end of each sentence. Write what type of sentence it is: *declarative, interrogative, imperative,* or *exclamatory*.

8. What day is it ____ _____

9. Go away ____ _____

10. The humidity weighed heavily on everyone ____ _____

Grammar Minutes · Grade 5 © 2009 Creative Teaching Press

Apply Your Grammar Knowledge

Minute 85

Name _____

For Numbers 1–3, underline the common nouns. Circle the proper nouns.

1. Seoul is the capital of South Korea.

2. When we went snorkeling in Waikiki, we saw a lot of fish.

3. The Lakers are my favorite basketball team.

For Numbers 4–7, write each noun in plural form.

4. manuscript _____

5. sketch _____

6. dragonfly _____

7. woman _____

For Numbers 8–10, rewrite each phrase in possessive form.

8. The pens belonging to the pigs _____

9. The howl of the wind _____

10. The curbs of the streets _____

Grammar Minutes · Grade 5 © 2009 Creative Teaching Press

Minute 86

Name _____

For Numbers 1–2, replace the underlined word(s) with a pronoun.

1. <u>Claude</u> enjoys riding his bike and playing tennis.   _____

2. <u>Paula and I</u> went fishing at the stream.   _____

For Numbers 3–7, circle the correct pronoun to complete each sentence.

3. Mr. Price asked Laura and (I/me) to deliver the package.

4. The blue and red skateboards belong to (we/us).

5. Tracy brought flowers for (her/she) and me.

6. (He/Him) and (I/me) will go to school on the bus.

7. I brought a release form for (her/she) so she could attend the field trip.

For Numbers 8–10, circle the pronoun in each sentence.

8. Everyone will make a ceramic bowl.

9. Will somebody please answer the door?

10. Anyone can play on the volleyball team.

Grammar Minutes · Grade 5 © 2009 Creative Teaching Press

Apply Your Grammar Knowledge

Minute 87

Name _____

For Numbers 1–5, replace the underlined word(s) with a pronoun.

1. The tabby cat cleaned <u>the tabby cat's</u> paw. _____

2. Jason and Brenda put on <u>Jason and Brenda's</u> uniforms. _____

3. We can fit two cars in <u>my family's</u> garage. _____

4. Lee always listens to <u>Mr. Daley's</u> radio program in the morning. _____

5. Dana wrote an essay and turned in <u>Dana's</u> paper in the morning. _____

For Numbers 6–10, circle the correct pronoun to complete each sentence.

6. "Kevin and Travis, keep your comments to _____."
yourselves yourself

7. The football fans showed their support by dressing _____ in school colors.
yourselves themselves

8. We looked at _____ in the photograph.
ourselves ourself

9. The man sat by _____ on the bench in the park.
itself himself

10. When Jenna fell on the rocks, she injured _____ badly.
herself themselves

Grammar Minutes · Grade 5 © 2009 Creative Teaching Press

Minute 88

Name _____

For Numbers 1–2, underline the verb in each sentence.

1. Right Away grocery store sells four different types of squash.

2. The Australian swimmer is the winner.

For Numbers 3–6, write each verb in past tense form.

Present Tense	Past Tense
3. begin	_____
4. expect	_____
5. wear	_____
6. decide	_____

For Numbers 7–10, circle the correct verb to complete each sentence.

7. Please (lay/lie) your bag on the bench.

8. The village men (sit/set) outside their huts in the evenings.

9. The sun (raises/rises) in the east.

10. The date to return the library books has (passed/past).

Apply Your Grammar Knowledge

Minute 89

Name _____

For Numbers 1–5, circle the correct verb form to complete each sentence.

1. Cats _____ chasing mice and birds.
   enjoy   enjoys

2. Ken and James _____ excellent writers.
   is   are

3. Dad _____ into the empty parking space.
   pull   pulls

4. There _____ dozens of bicycles locked in the rack.
   were   was

5. Daisy _____ to finish her book report tonight.
   hope   hopes

For Numbers 6–10, circle the correct pronoun to complete each sentence.

6. Girls can store P.E. clothes in (their/her) lockers.

7. Pilots must train extensively before earning (their/his) licenses.

8. Any girl who finishes early may work on (her/their) homework.

9. The doctors finished (their/his) rounds and went home.

10. We ran away fast when we saw the skunk lift
    (their/its) tail.

Grammar Minutes · Grade 5 © 2009 Creative Teaching Press

Minute 90

Name _____

Circle the correct form of the adjective to complete each sentence.

1. Chocolate ice cream is (more good/better) than vanilla.

2. The Metro Maple Leafs are the (worse/worst) team in the entire league.

3. The Bucking Bronco roller coaster is (more exciting/most exciting) than the Free Fall ride.

4. Which jar has (most/more) coffee?

5. The (most creative/more creative) designer in the contest will win a new car.

6. The overhead light is the (brighter/brightest) light in the entire room.

7. It is (more colder/colder) in Alaska than in Florida.

8. That is the (weirder/weirdest) insect I've ever seen.

9. The student with the (most clever/cleverest) idea will win the prize.

10. A gold medal is awarded to the (most good/best) contestant in the Academic Decathlon.

Apply Your Grammar Knowledge

Minute 91

Name _____

For Numbers 1–5, circle the word the underlined adverb modifies.

1. Jonah waited <u>eagerly</u> for his appointment.

2. The boat bounced <u>roughly</u> on the wide blue sea.

3. The ballerina twirled <u>daintily</u> on her pointe shoes.

4. Bring it <u>tomorrow</u>.

5. Raindrops trickled <u>slowly</u> down the windowpane.

For Numbers 6–10, write what question the underlined adverb answers: *how, when, where, how often* or *to what degree.*

6. Monica exercises <u>regularly</u>.   _____

7. Mrs. Petersen said to put the boxes <u>here</u>.   _____

8. Dogs barked <u>noisily</u> as we rode past.   _____

9. Charge the battery <u>fully</u> before using.   _____

10. The wind blew the snow <u>sideways</u>.   _____

Grammar Minutes · Grade 5 © 2009 Creative Teaching Press

Minute 92

Name _____

For Numbers 1–3, write either *between* or *among* to correctly complete each sentence.

1. The race will be _____ Jerome and Taylor.

2. It is difficult to choose _____ the many flavors.

3. Cross the street _____ the yellow lines at the crosswalk.

For Numbers 4–10, circle the preposition(s) in each sentence.

4. The television in the living room is still not working.

5. The table under the window provides the best light for reading.

6. Gravel crunched under our feet as we walked up the driveway.

7. Maria poured juice into a tall glass.

8. Bart will play the lead role, Julius Caesar, in the school play.

9. Darlene waited all day for the dough to rise.

10. Walk around the lake and stop at the path's end.

Apply Your Grammar Knowledge

Minute 93

Name _____

For Numbers 1–3, underline the appositive in each sentence. Circle the noun phrase or pronoun it describes.

1. Wendy, my older sister, attends Willowbrook High School.

2. The prime minister, a well-respected man, made the decision to raise taxes.

3. The first woman to scale Mt. Everest, Junko Tabei of Japan, accomplished a remarkable achievement.

For Numbers 4–7, write *D* if the underlined clause is a dependent clause or *I* if the clause is an independent clause

4. The red roses in Mrs. Rueben's yard are so beautiful in the summer. ____

5. Our team won the basketball game, and we felt proud of our success. ____

6. Maddy makes jewelry, and she often gives it to her friends. ____

7. Mom hung blue curtains in my bedroom to block the morning light. ____

For Numbers 8–10, write a dependent clause to make each sentence a complex sentence.

8. The temperature outside is very cold _____.

9. Wash thoroughly with soap _____.

10. The newspaper reported a robbery _____.

Grammar Minutes · Grade 5 © 2009 Creative Teaching Press

Minute 94

Name _____

Write *Yes* if the sentence is written correctly. Write *No* if it is not.

1. We don't got any money to buy a movie ticket. _____

2. It's so foggy I can't barely see anything. _____

3. We could not go to the park because it was raining. _____

4. Lisa and Benjamin don't never miss hockey practice. _____

5. Atlantic Avenue is nowhere around here. _____

6. Our mother just told us that we did not have to
   clean the living room. _____

7. She don't have no pen I can borrow. _____

8. Do not forget to close the door behind you. _____

9. I was not going to not do my homework. _____

10. I have not seen Sherry anywhere. _____

Apply Your Grammar Knowledge

Minute 95

Name _____

Write a synonym and an antonym for each word.

Word	Synonym	Antonym
1. precious	_____	_____
2. messy	_____	_____
3. alike	_____	_____
4. many	_____	_____
5. sharp	_____	_____
6. active	_____	_____
7. dangerous	_____	_____
8. quiet	_____	_____
9. wide	_____	_____
10. brave	_____	_____

Grammar Minutes · Grade 5 © 2009 Creative Teaching Press

Minute 96

Name _____

For Numbers 1–5, complete each sentence with the correct homophone from the box.

reign/rein/rain   pear/pair   plain/plane   ceiling/sealing   guest/guessed

1. When the _____ began, Lindsey opened her umbrella.

2. The _____ was painted a bright blue.

3. Alex sliced the _____ and brought it to the table.

4. The students _____ how many buttons were in the jar.

5. The animals roamed the African _____.

For Numbers 6–10, write the homograph to complete each sentence.
(**Hint:** The word is used in the sentence.)

6. I object to having that _____ in my backpack.

7. Can you please place your _____ in the recycling bin?

8. The spring rains have made the _____ water plentiful.

9. What can you produce from the items in the _____ section of the grocery store?

10. Who will conduct the orchestra if her _____ is unacceptable?

Grammar Minutes · Grade 5 © 2009 Creative Teaching Press

Apply Your Grammar Knowledge

Minute 97

Name _____

For Numbers 1–5, add a suffix to change the meaning of each word. Use each suffix in the box only once.

-ness	-ible	-ish	-ly	-en

1. sincere _____

2. bright _____

3. quick _____

4. self _____

5. flex _____

For Numbers 6–10, add a prefix to each word and write its definition. Use each prefix in the box only once.

pre-	un-	in-	im-	dis-

Word with Prefix   **Definition**

6. _____ similar   _____

7. _____ comfortable   _____

8. _____ fix   _____

9. _____ visible   _____

10. _____ possible   _____

Grammar Minutes · Grade 5 © 2009 Creative Teaching Press

Minute 98

Name _____

For Numbers 1–4, draw a line from the Latin or Greek root to its meaning. Draw another line from the meaning to the sample word.

Root	Definition	New Word
1. ology •	• study of •	• biography
2. port •	• water •	• geology
3. aqua •	• writing •	• portable
4. graph •	• to carry •	• aquarium

For Numbers 5–7, add a prefix to change the meaning of each word. Use the prefixes in the box.

5. _____ port

6. _____ word

7. _____ wind

re-	fore-	trans-

For Numbers 8–10, add a suffix to change the meaning of each word. Use the suffixes in the box.

8. graph _____

9. flavor _____

10. profess _____

-ful	-or	-ic

Apply Your Grammar Knowledge

Grammar Minutes · Grade 5 © 2009 Creative Teaching Press

Minute 99

Name _____

Circle all the words that need to be capitalized in each sentence.

1. Wall Street is a street located near South street Seaport in New York city.

2. Before it became the financial center of the united states, Wall Street was the center of government.

3. New York was the capital of early america, and all the government offices were located on Wall Street.

4. george washington was inaugurated in the city of New York.

5. Many impressive buildings make up the Wall street neighborhood.

6. Federal hall and the trump towers are landmark buildings on Wall Street.

7. The New York stock exchange is one of the most important buildings in the city.

8. The site where the World Trade Center stood prior to september 11, 2001, is slated to become the Freedom tower.

9. If you ever have the chance to visit our nation's former capital, take the opportunity. Then compare the city life between washington, d.c., and New York.

10. Many people mistakenly believe that New York City is the capital of new york state, but the capital is actually albany. This mistake just shows how important New York City is!

Grammar Minutes · Grade 5 © 2009 Creative Teaching Press

Minute 100

Name _____

Insert commas and end punctuation in the correct places in each sentence.

1. The tropical rain forests of South America Africa and Southeast Asia are always warm and wet

2. Animals such as birds and bats live in the rain forests

3. Did you know many animals in the tropical rain forest live in trees

4. Mom said "Pack up kids we're going to Water World"

5. An hour later there were eight of us in the van

6. The trip to Water World takes over an hour so we sang songs on the way

7. We went on the junior slides the taller slides and the slippery slope but no one dared go on the Wild Riot

8. "That was the most fun I ever had" exclaimed Robert

9. "Can we go again" asked Vanessa

10. Later after all of us were in bed we talked about all of the fun we had

Apply Your Grammar Knowledge

Minute Answer Key

Minute 1
1. C
2. I
3. I
4. C
5. I
6. C
7. I
8. C
9. C
10. I

Minute 2
1. Ella
2. squid
3. stars
4. Petronas Towers
5. phones
6. painted
7. is
8. sway
9. is awarded
10. came

Minute 3
1. My sister Lindsey
2. The brand-new building
3. Alex's sister
4. The elementary school students
5. The eager group of tourists
6. put his books in my backpack
7. is a fun winter sport
8. helped the flowers bloom
9. politely handed me my receipt
10. will take her place

Minute 4
1. Gretchen and Thelma
2. roses and daisies
3. Sweaters, coats, and rugs
4. The guard and the center
5. The United States, Canada, and Mexico
For Numbers 6–10, answers will vary. Sample answers include:
6. wiped
7. splashed
8. downloaded
9. washes
10. pack

Minute 5
1. circle: Look at that! underline: Isn't that a gorgeous sunset?
2. circle: I can't believe I missed the bus! underline: What will I do now?
3. circle: It's unbelievable! underline: Was that your fastest swim record?
4. circle: I can't believe it's broken! underline: How long will it be before we can get it repaired?
5. !, ,?
6. !, ?
7. ?, !, . or !
For Numbers 8–10, answers will vary. Sample answers include:
8. I'm so hungry!
9. Please lower your voices!
10. You really have to try this!

Minute 6
1. I
2. D
3. I
4. I
5. D
6. I
7. D
8. I
9. I
10. D

Minute 7
1. .
2. ?
3. .
4. !
5. ?
6. .
7. !
8. .
9. .
10. ?

Minute 8
1. .
2. .
3. .
4. I
5. .
6. I
7. I
8. .
9. I
10. I

Minute 9
1. S
2. P
3. P
4. P
5. P
6. S
7. S
8. P
9. S
10. P

Minute 10
1. circle: virus underline: A virus
2. circle: Great Egyptian Pyramids underline: The Great Egyptian Pyramids
3. circle: Heather and Tony underline: My good friends Heather and Tony
4. circle: robin underline: The bright red robin
5. circle: hot chocolate underline: The steaming hot chocolate

For Numbers 6–10, answers will vary. Sample answers include:
6. Martin walked to school and pulled open the school doors.
7. All plants use oxygen and take in water.
8. My mother washed and curled her hair.
9. Many Brazilians love to watch and play soccer.
10. Rachel strolled along the boardwalk and looked at the view.

Minute 11
1. ., D
2. ?, I
3. !, E
4. ., IMP
5. ?, I
6. ., IMP
7. ., D
8. ?, I
9. !, E
10. ., D

Minute 12
Order of answers within each category may vary.
Person
1. explorer
2. veterinarian
3. woman
Place
4. city
5. park
6. post office
Thing or idea
7. bread
8. liberty
9. bucket
10. friendship

Minute 13
1. underline: friends circle: Jeff, Onondaga Camp
2. underline: glove circle: Javier
3. underline: game circle: Central Park
4. underline: students, causes circle: Revolutionary War
5. underline: ingredients circle: Steven
6. underline: house circle: Nick's
7. underline: teacher circle: Hyde's Planetarium
8. underline: day circle: Byron Elementary School
9. underline: president circle: United States, White House
10. underline: pictures

circle: Venus

Minute 14
1. Brazil
2. Budapest
3. Chinese
4. Diwali
5. Eiffel Tower
6. Torah
7. Muslims
8. Vatican City
9. Juanita
10. Walt Disney Concert Hall

Minute 15
1. shoes
2. heroes
3. boxes
4. skates
5. monkeys
6. companies
7. princesses
8. cherries
9. witches
10. chimneys

Minute 16
1. children, places
2. photos, deer
3. dishes, potatoes
4. families, blessings
5. sheep, hills
6. pens, shelves
7. leaves, piles
8. friends, quizzes
9. doors, elves
10. movies, biographies

Minute 17
1. The spider's web
2. Teresa's cookie
3. Kenneth's flute
4. The student's lunch
5. The doctor's stethoscope
6. The child's father
7. Ann's shoes
8. The map's legend
9. The team's mascot
10. The writer's biography

Minute 18
1. The boys' team
2. The teachers' lounge
3. The ships' captains
4. The stores' computers
5. The children's classroom
6. The women's dresses
7. The partners' projects
8. The leaves' colors
9. The oxen's harnesses
10. The deer's hooves

Minute Answer Key

Minute 19
1. He
2. They
3. She
4. He
5. They
6. us
7. her, me
8. us
9. her, me
10. him, me

Minute 20
1. myself
2. himself
3. yourselves
4. itself
5. ourselves
6. her
7. my, his
8. Whose
9. mine
10. Your

Minute 21
1. who
2. that
3. who
4. that
5. who
6. Anyone
7. anything
8. somebody
9. everyone
10. Each

Minute 22
1. they are
2. their
3. her
4. his
5. their
6. its
7. their
8. her
9. they are
10. they

Minute 23
1. underline: sandwich
   circle: Charlene
2. underline: guitar
   circle: Melody Music Shop
3. underline: birthday
   circle: Parker's, January
4. underline: race
   circle: Tour de France, France
5. underline: theater
   circle: Monday
6. underline: squirrel, trees
   circle: Highland Park
7. underline: apartment, floor
   circle: None
8. underline: banker, loan
   circle: Louise
9. underline: None
   circle: Statue of Liberty, New York City
10. underline: garbage
    circle: None

Minute 24
For Numbers 1–5, order of answers may vary.
1. climbers
2. knives
3. utensils
4. months
5. people
6. beetles
7. hobbies
8. mice
9. halves
10. echoes

Minute 25
1. men's department
2. Cindy's bookshelf
3. galleries' windows
4. kindergartner's crayons
5. runners' water bottles
6. underline: Melissa's motorcycle
   circle: friends' motorcycles
7. underline: Dad's day
   circle: Dolphins' victory
8. underline: Jessica's allergies
   circle: flowers' pollen
9. underline: Daria's Grocery Store
   circle: dogs' loud barking
10. underline: Lisa's pet hamster
    circle: sofas' slippery cushions

Minute 26
1. me
2. her
3. them
4. her, him
5. him, me
6. He
7. It
8. It
9. They
10. We

Minute 27
1. his
2. Their or His or Her or Our
3. their
4. her
5. our
6. himself
7. herself
8. themselves
9. yourself
10. itself

Minute 28
1. who
2. that
3. that
4. that
5. who
6. No
7. Yes
8. No
9. No
10. Yes

Minute 29
Answers for second verb will vary.
1. soars, flies
2. drives, travels
3. sparkle, twinkle
4. leaps, bounds
5. skate, blade
6. cuts, gathers
7. lost, misplaced
8. sails, floats
9. swims, explores
10. hit, batted

Minute 30
1. is
2. am
3. are
4. are
5. were
6. a
7. b
8. b
9. b
10. a

Minute 31
1. sailed
2. screamed
3. flew
4. answered
5. grew
6. acted
7. wore
8. wrote
9. boiled
10. broke

Minute 32
1. invented
2. hunted
3. joking
4. mentioned
5. moving
6. offering
7. ruled
8. planning
9. unloading
10. visiting

Minute 33
1. lay
2. lies
3. set
4. sit
5. rise
6. raised
7. lay
8. passed
9. sat
10. lay

Minute 34
1. I laugh, You laugh, She laughs, They laugh
2. I ask, You ask, He asks, They ask
3. I start, You start, It starts, They start
4. I paint, You paint, He paints, They paint
5. I dance, You dance, She dances, They dance
6. mop
7. plants
8. stings
9. turns
10. ignores

Minute 35
1. is
2. earns
3. is
4. are
5. are
6. are
7. are
8. drives
9. wear
10. are

Minute 36
1. circle: raced
2. circle: melts
3. underline: was
4. circle: built
5. underline: is
For Numbers 6–10, answers will vary. Sample answers include:
6. The snow fell from the dark sky.
7. The sun is shining down on the buildings.
8. My friend and I laughed and danced at the concert.
9. Lisa yawned and stretched.
10. My stomach grumbled loudly.

Minute 37
1. H
2. L
3. L
4. H
5. H
6. H
7. L
8. H
9. L
10. L

Minute 38
1. ran
2. dove
3. froze
4. walked
5. thought
6. sweeping
7. dried
8. marching
9. stretched
10. exploded

Minute 39
1. lay
2. lie
3. set
4. passed
5. raise
6. Yes
7. No
8. No
9. Yes
10. No

Minute 40
1. expects
2. flops
3. were
4. are
5. plans
6. is
7. wishes
8. eats
9. are
10. uses

Minute 41
1. awkward
2. magic
3. delicious
4. tiny, black, white
5. dirty, smelly
6. unpredictable
7. beautiful
8. demanding
9. little, green
10. mashed

Minute 42
1. helpful or kind
2. dangerous
3. exquisite
4. speedy
5. plump or immense
6. contented
7. level
8. helpful or kind
9. immense
10. playful

Minute 43
1. smoother
2. fresher
3. more general
4. more difficult
5. more jealous
6. kinder

Minute Answer Key

7. lighter
8. more memorable
9. quicker
10. more helpless

Minute 44
1. best
2. worse
3. more
4. less
5. worse
6. flatter, flattest
7. braver, bravest
8. stronger, strongest
9. calmer, calmest
10. leaner, leanest

Minute 45
1. mightily
2. heavily
3. eagerly
4. exactly
5. crazily
6. good
7. well
8. good
9. well
10. well

Minute 46
1. how
2. how often
3. to what degree
4. when
5. where
6. when
7. how
8. how
9. how often
10. to what degree

Minute 47
1. faster, fastest
2. more quietly, most quietly
3. earlier, earliest
4. more often, most often
5. more slowly, most slowly
6. farther, farthest
7. nearer, nearest
8. more carefully, most carefully
9. sooner, soonest
10. more gracefully, most gracefully

Minute 48
1. harder   6. best
2. larger   7. worse
3. louder   8. least
4. smallest   9. fewer
5. tallest   10. most

Minute 49
1. ate
2. held
3. go
4. held
5. considered
6. sat
7. spoke
8. marched
9. generous
10. remember

Minute 50
1. adv   6. adv
2. adj   7. adj
3. adv   8. adj
4. adj   9. adj
5. adv   10. adv

Minute 51
1. seat
2. shone
3. view
4. rhythm
5. runs
6. signs
7. climbed
8. bounced
9. worked
10. traveler

Minute 52
1. between, as
2. with, inside
3. at, across
4. at, after
5. beside, up
6. inside
7. near
8. beneath
9. with
10. Since

Minute 53
1. between   6. No
2. among   7. Yes
3. between   8. No
4. between   9. Yes
5. between   10. No

Minute 54
1. a   6. b
2. b   7. a
3. b   8. b
4. b   9. b
5. a   10. b

Minute 55
For Numbers 1–5, answers will vary.
6. inside the box
7. on my desk
8. through the window

9. to the party
10. on the sidewalk

Minute 56
1. a   6. the
2. an   7. the, a
3. an   8. The
4. a   9. an, the
5. an   10. a, an

Minute 57
1. so
2. and
3. However
4. but
5. and
For Numbers 6–10, answers will vary.
6. yet
7. and
8. but
9. or
10 Although

Minute 58
For Numbers 1–4, answers will vary.
Sample answers include:
1. I will go to the park and get Jerome.
2. Veronica enjoys ballet, although she doesn't like ballet recitals.
3. The guitarist played a quiet ballad, and the singer hummed softly.
4. The Internet is a good source of information and entertainment.
5. No   8. No
6. No   9. Yes
7. No   10. Yes

Minute 59
1. underline: the soccer star
   circle: Jake
2. underline: my pediatrician
   circle: Dr. Williams
3. underline: Roald Dahl's masterpiece
   circle: Charlie and the Chocolate Factory
4. underline: Hannah
   circle: sister
5. underline: the epitome of American racing
   circle: Indianapolis 500 race
6. I
7. D
8. D
9. I
10. D

Minute 60
1. to the performance
2. on earth
3. in the 1960s
4. in the Bahamas
5. for our family
6. in our community
7. by the musician
8. of the library, into the bright sunshine
9. on a farm, in West Virginia
10. in 1945, after World War II ended

Minute 61
1. a   6. the
2. a   7. a
3. a   8. the
4. an   9. A
5. a   10. an

Minute 62
1. yet
2. because
3. but also
4. or
5. and
6. circle: and
7. underline: so
8. underline: or
9. circle: and
10. underline: although

Minute 63
1. Yes   4. No
2. Yes   5. Yes
3. No   6. No
For Numbers 7–10, Answers will vary.
Sample answers include:
7. At summer's end, many students pack up for college and drive to their campuses.
8. The pizza was cut into eight pieces, and it was all gone shortly thereafter.
9. The athletes in the triathlon run, bike for miles, and swim.
10. My friend and I know how to ride a bicycle and a unicycle.

Minute 64
Numbers 1–5, answers will vary.
6. D
7. I
8. D
9. D
10. I

Minute Answer Key

Minute 65
Answers will vary. Sample answers include:
1. airport
2. backtrack
3. brainstorm
4. someday
5. doghouse
6. sweetheart
7. countertop
8. downtown
9. earthquake
10. manhole

Minute 66
Answers will vary. Sample answers include:
1. noisy
2. fearful
3. limit
4. worried
5. height
6. filthy
7. gorgeous
8. gleaming
9. endlessly
10. breezy

Minute 67
Answers will vary. Sample answers include:
1. intelligent
2. thin
3. separated
4. fight
5. middle
6. terrible
7. bashful
8. stinky
9. adorable
10. trail

Minute 68
1. whole
2. criticize
3. ancient
4. floor
5. slow
6. unsheltered
7. subtract
8. intermittent
9. awake
10. rough

Minute 69
Answers will vary. Sample answers include:
1. early
2. ancient
3. fresh
4. plentiful
5. mountainous
6. unlocked
7. rise
8. diligent
9. full
10. trustworthy

Minute 70
Answers will vary. Sample answers include:
1. I live close to school.
2. The bass from the stereo made the house shake.
3. Gerald dove from the board into the water.
4. Our house is two stories tall.
5. We need food and water to live.
6. The girls had separate rooms.
7. This year in science we have two major projects.
8. After he slammed his finger in the door, his eyes began to tear up.
9. The president of the company came to address the crowd.
10. For my birthday, the only present I want is a skateboard.

Minute 71
1. ate   6. principal
2. cereal   7. groan
3. heard   8. passed
4. maid   9. bear
5. role   10. mist

Minute 72
1. to   6. their
2. two   7. They're
3. too   8. It's
4. Too   9. you're
5. There   10. its

Minute 73
Answers will vary. Sample answers include:
1. synonym: exhausted
   antonym: energetic
2. synonym: alike
   antonym: dissimilar
3. synonym: loud
   antonym: quiet
4. synonym: accept
   antonym: give
5. synonym: funny
   antonym: serious
6. synonym: enlarge
   antonym: lessen
7. synonym: saunter
   antonym: scurry
8. synonym: same
   antonym: imbalanced
9. synonym: brave

   antonym: cowardly
10. synonym: sadness
    antonym: elation

Minute 74
1. present   6. course
2. wound   7. kernel
3. minute   8. feat
4. contract   9. knight
5. desert   10. allowed

Minute 75
1. No   6. No
2. No   7. Yes
3. No   8. No
4. No   9. Yes
5. Yes   10. Yes

Minute 76
1. they have   6. You'll
2. she had or   7. doesn't
   she would   8. Let's
3. I am   9. Who'd
4. do not   10. won't
5. had not

Minute 77
1. Pedro, please remember to buy milk, butter, and eggs.
2. Yes, I
3. Marie Curie, a Nobel Prize winner, was
4. anytime, but   8. No
5. head, thorax, and   9. Yes
6. Yes   10. Yes
7. No

Minute 78
Answers will vary. Sample answers include:
1. ~~no~~, any (or, ~~no~~ without an additional word)
2. ~~no~~, any
3. ~~can't~~, can (or, ~~hardly~~)
4. ~~barely~~ (or, ~~couldn't~~, could)
5. ~~never~~, (or, ~~can't~~, can)
6. ~~not~~
7. ~~nobody~~, anybody
8. ~~nothing~~, anything
9. ~~nothing~~, anything (or, ~~isn't~~, is)
10. ~~never~~ ~~nothing~~, anything (or, ~~aren't~~ are, ~~nothing~~, anything)

Minute 79
1. Tony Hawk was born May 12, 1968, in San Diego, California.
2. Tokyo, Japan, is one of the world's most populous cities.
3. Jayden said, "You make the best chocolate pudding in the world."

4. The National Baseball Hall of Fame is located in Cooperstown, New York.
5. "I watched the funniest program on television," Michael said.
6. Until the bridge is completed, we will have to cross at the intersection down the street.
7. The storm clouds began to gather, and we ran for cover in the cellar.
8. Quinn, will you please answer questions three, four, and five for us?
9. Keisha, the tallest girl in the class, balanced herself carefully on a chair and pinned the picture to the bulletin board.
10. My three favorite Olympic sports are swimming, basketball, and gymnastics.

Minute 80
Answers will vary. Sample answers include:
1. nonprofit, not for gain
2. overeat, consume too much
3. foresight, see before
4. mishandle, manage badly
5. review, to look at again
6. antiseptic, against infection
7. disagree, not think alike
8. international, among nations
9. submarine, underwater
10. transport, carry to another place

Minute 81
1. affordable   6. poetic
2. courageous   7. actor
3. hopeful   8. movement
4. sharpest   9. helpless
5. wooden   10. fruity

Minute 82
1. dent, tooth, dentures
2. aud, hear, audio
3. bio, life, biology
4. cred, trust, credible
5. circ, around, circulate
6. graph, writing, graphic
7. prim, first, primary
8. voc, call, vocal
9. cap, take, capture
10. scope, see, microscope

Minute 83
1. dent   6. anti-, -ic
2. bio, chem 7. -able
3. circ   8. sub-
4. aud   9. -less
5. tele, scope 10. -ment

Minute Answer Key

Minute 84
1. underline: Babies
   circle: cry
2. underline: The swimmers
   circle: raced to the finish line
3. underline: The city of Los Angeles
   circle: hosted the 1984 Olympic Games
4. underline: A rusty old car
   circle: sat abandoned on the side of the road
5. No
6. Yes
7. No
8. ?, interrogative
9. !, exclamatory
10. ., declarative

Minute 85
1. underline: capital
   circle: Seoul, South Korea
2. underline: snorkeling, fish
   circle: Waikiki
3. underline: team
   circle: Lakers
4. manuscripts
5. sketches
6. dragonflies
7. women
8. pigs' pens
9. wind's howl
10. streets' curbs

Minute 86
1. He
2. We
3. me
4. us
5. her
6. He, I
7. her
8. Everyone
9. somebody
10. Anyone

Minute 87
1. its
2. their
3. our
4. his
5. her
6. yourselves
7. themselves
8. ourselves
9. himself
10. herself

Minute 88
1. sells
2. is
3. began
4. expected
5. wore
6. decided
7. lay
8. sit
9. rises
10. passed

Minute 89
1. enjoy
2. are
3. pulls
4. were
5. hopes
6. their
7. their
8. her
9. their
10. its

Minute 90
1. better
2. worst
3. more exciting
4. more
5. most creative
6. brightest
7. colder
8. weirdest
9. cleverest
10. best

Minute 91
1. waited
2. bounced
3. twirled
4. Bring
5. trickled
6. how often
7. where
8. how
9. to what degree
10. how

Minute 92
1. between
2. among
3. between
4. in
5. under, for
6. under, up
7. into
8. in
9. for
10. around, at

Minute 93
1. underline: my older sister
   circle: Wendy
2. underline: a well-respected man
   circle: The prime minister
3. underline: Junko Tabei of Japan
   circle: The first woman to scale Mt. Everest
4. D
5. I

6. I
7. D
For Numbers 8–10, answers will vary. Sample answers include:
8. The temperature outside is very cold when it's winter.
9. Wash thoroughly with soap before handling food.
10. The newspaper reported a robbery in the west part of town.

Minute 94
1. No
2. No
3. Yes
4. No
5. Yes
6. Yes
7. No
8. Yes
9. No
10. Yes

Minute 95
Answers will vary. Sample answers include:
1. synonym: prized
   antonym: worthless
2. synonym: cluttered
   antonym: neat
3. synonym: same
   antonym: dissimilar
4. synonym: numerous
   antonym: few
5. synonym: spiky
   antonym: blunt
6. synonym: energetic
   antonym: idle
7. synonym: hazardous
   antonym: safe
8. synonym: silent
   antonym: loud
9. synonym: broad
   antonym: narrow
10. synonym: heroic
    antonym: spinele...

Minute 96
1. rain
2. ceiling
3. pear
4. guessed
5. plain
6. obj...
7. can...
8. sprin...
9. produ...
10. conduc...

Minute 97
1. sincerely or sincereness
2. brighten, brightness, or brightly
3. quickness, quicken, or quickly
4. selfish or selfness
5. flexible
For Numbers 6–10, answers will vary. Sample answers include:
6. dissimilar, not the same
7. uncomfortable, not at ease
8. prefix, something set before

9. invisible, not able to be seen
10. impossible, not able to do

Minute 98
1. study of, geology
2. to carry, portable
3. water, aquarium
4. writing, biography
5. transport
6. foreword
7. rewind
8. graphic
9. flavorful
10. professor

Minute 99
1. Street, City
2. United States
3. America
4. George Washington
5. Street
6. Hall, Trump Towers
7. Stock Exchange
8. September, Tower
9. Washington, D.C.
10. New York State, Albany

Minute 100
1. The tropical rain forests of South America, Africa, and Southeast Asia are always warm and wet.
2. Animals such as birds and bats live in the rain forests.
3. Did you know many animals in the tropical rain forest live in trees?
4. Mom said, "Pack up, kids. We're going to Water World!"
5. An hour later, there were eight of us in the van.
6. The trip to Water World takes over an hour, so we sang songs on the way.
7. We went on the junior slides, the taller slides, and the slippery slope, but no one dared go on the Wild Riot.
8. "That was the most fun I ever had!" exclaimed Robert.
9. "Can we go again?" asked Vanessa.
10. Later, after all of us were in bed, we talked about all of the fun we had.